MW00593161

Clarify, Construct, and Control Your Career

Practical Principles To Help You Develop And
Advance Your Career.

Edgar Butler, Jr.

EDGARBUTLERJR.COM

Disclaimer

The information published in this book represents the opinions, personal research, business and career experience of the author. Since the success of anyone depends upon the skill and ability of the person, the author makes no guarantees and disclaims any personal loss or liabilities that may occur as a result of the use of the information contained herein.

This publication is designed to provide accurate and authoritative information in regard to the subject matter covered in it. It is provided with the understanding that the publisher is not engaged in rendering legal, accounting, or other professional services. If legal advice or other expert assistance is required, the services of a competent professional person should be sought.

TABLE OF CONTENTS

Purpose in Your Position

Many people desire to be in a different place in their professional career and personal life. There was a point in my life that I began to reject my employment because I felt it was not where I was going. I knew God was taking me to a place that would allow me to speak and coach full-time, so I rejected the association of my employment with my speaking and coaching business. I thought if people knew I had a full-time job they wouldn't look at me as a speaker or coach. God showed me I was rejecting the very audience He gave me to hone my skills. I understand there is purpose in my position; I'm around over 400 people daily, and I have the opportunity to motivate, inspire, and coach them each day. I began to look at every day as an opportunity to add value to the people and environment around me.

When I have someone that comes to my desk who wants to discuss life and not just numbers, I understand that is my coaching client. No, I don't get to process a payment for our session, but I do get to fulfill purpose through our session. When I have meetings with teams throughout the week and they are looking for me to give them some motivation, I give them the same passion and fire I would give a paying client, because I understand that is my audience. No, I don't get to give them an invoice after I speak, but I use the opportunity to add value to my environment and at the same time I sharpen my skills. Again, I realize there is purpose in my position.

Maybe you have also had these feelings. I want to provide you with a word of encouragement. Do not reject, regret, or neglect where you are just because it's not the place you are going. Understand the purpose in your position. Whatever your current employment, from delivery driver to Vice President, cashier to business owner, understand there is purpose in your position. Your customers are your audience and clients. You should look to add value each day to the lives of the people you meet, work with, and serve. Whether it's 1 or 100, for free or for a fee, your energy, passion, and service should always be the same, 100%!

Lessons Learned

As a leader working in a structured work environment I've spent a lot of time leading, talking to, counseling, mentoring and coaching employees. I see so many employees who are working below their talent and skill-level and they are not taking full advantage of the opportunities afforded to them by their employer. I was in this same boat at one point in my career. I thought opportunities should have been given to me just because I was doing o.k. in my position. Again, I was doing o.k.; however, I wasn't giving maximum effort in every area, but I was expecting maximum reward.

I didn't put myself in the most favorable position in the eyes of leadership, and after an unfortunate misunderstanding, I was fired. I put my family in a tough situation financially and emotionally. Due to my daughter's medical condition (discussed in a later chapter), my termination made things financially uncomfortable for a while. I said to myself I would never put my family in a position like that again. This was the beginning of my relentless effort to create legacy and a solid foundation for my family, and to take full advantage of every opportunity afforded to me when it came to my career.

If you are currently not where you think you

should be or where you want to be in your career, this is the book for you! Throughout this book I will give you practical principles that will help you position yourself to develop and advance your career. This book can serve as your guide, but how far you go and what you achieve will fully depend on your effort, determination, ambition, and drive. So, my first question for you is how bad do you want it?

1
MAKE A DECISION!

"If you want to make a difference, you have to make a decision." – Dr Eric Thomas

When it comes to having success, it doesn't matter what area of your life you choose. Whether personal or professional, it all begins with a decision. What I have come to realize is that the lack of effort to pursue something better stops most people from truly pursuing their dreams. Most get discouraged after one or two attempts. So, while those that are successful continue to pursue their goals, those that aren't successful have decided to not continue the pursuit.

I remember working at Publix warehouse and feeling as if I wanted to do more, and that I could do more. Although I wanted to leave, I hadn't made a decision to leave. It was like I was impatiently waiting for the job that I wanted to come find me! I could be wrong, but I've never known that to happen to anyone. So, while I grew more and more miserable, something occurred that changed the way I viewed working for the rest of my life. I was fired! I couldn't believe it! Me….. fired?

I had heard about people being fired, and I knew people that had been fired, but I never thought it could happen to me. I truly believe that because I was not willing to make a decision, God closed the door and made the decision for me. It was time to move. As much as I hated going to this job, I wouldn't leave because I was comfortable. I had a steady paycheck, and I knew what I was doing. I think that being miserable but comfortable is one of the most dangerous positions to be in.

Being fired is definitely not the best feeling in the world, but for me it is a part of my story which helped shape me into the person I am today. I don't regret it, but I don't suggest it. If you are having these same feelings about your current job, you have to get to a place where you are ready to make a decision to pursue better.

One thing I can say is that I developed a strong work ethic while working at Publix. I was working five, and sometimes six days a week. The days were long, 10 and 12 hours most days. To top it off, it was all physical labor. Every day, we would go in and race against the clock, and against each other. I wanted to be the fastest, so every day I went in, I pushed myself beyond what I thought were my mental and physical limits. Although being fired was not the best feeling in the world, I chose to look at the positives that I gained from my time there. It's easy to remember and dwell on the negative experiences, but I encourage you to pull out the positives and turn your challenges into triumphs that will help you as you move towards your career goals.

1. Let go of any negative work experiences you have been holding on to, and list some positive lessons and attributes you've learned about yourself in your previous and/or current roles.

_____

_____

_____

_____

2. How can you use those lessons to help you become more productive and/or advance in your current or future role?

_____

_____

_____

_____

A few months after being fired, I was hired at Rooms To Go warehouse. I accepted this job with a chip on my shoulder. I had 7 ½ years of warehouse experience and a two-year degree. I knew other people that were in leadership positions, who didn't have as much experience as I had in that type of environment, and they didn't have a college degree. I thought that I should have been brought in at a leadership level, but

I told myself that I was going to outwork everyone around me to prove to them I deserved to be in leadership.

I knew the work ethic I developed from working at Publix was going to serve me well going forward. I asked the Rooms To Go leadership team how long I had to be there before I could start applying for leadership positions. They told me six months. I set a six-month goal towards placing myself in position to start applying for leadership. I went to work every day ready to prove myself. I exceeded the expectations that were set, and I made myself visible. I researched what their leadership role consisted of, and I began to exhibit those characteristics in my current role. I understood how to position myself for advancement within the structure, and I did just that. As a result, I was promoted to leadership during my seventh month in the company. Additionally, I had developed an understanding of the requirements for career advancement.

1. **Determine a goal you want to accomplish in your career.**

2. Do you know what it takes to accomplish that goal?

_____

3. If your answer to question 2 is no, for the next week, I want you to research what it takes to attain the goal you set in question one and write out what you learned.

_____

_____

_____

_____

_____

_____

_____

_____

4. If your answer to question 2 is yes, what steps can you take today to start working towards the goal you set in question 1?

_____

_____

_____

_____

I stayed at Rooms to Go for about 5 ½ years and the desire for wanting to do more started to show up again. I always knew I had what it took to be successful in the corporate world, but I never pursued the opportunity. At the urging of my mother, I applied to State Farm.

Finally, I landed a job in Corporate America. The funny thing is, this was the career I always wanted but I hadn't made a decision to pursue it until years after I was fired from a job I hated.

After I began working in the corporate world, I started having regrets that I hadn't pursued this dream sooner. I overcame those feelings and decided not to allow that stop me from getting to the position I wanted, which was leadership. Leadership was my goal and on day one, I made a decision that I would get there. I was brought in at an entry level position, and I achieved my goal in 5 ½ years with the company. I've led teams responsible for managing multi-million dollar books of business for the No. 1 P&C Insurer in the United States. And it all started with me making a decision.

Pursuing your lifelong dream, a better relationship, a better marriage, or a certain professional career all starts with making a decision to go after those things. You have to decide to go after your lifelong dream; you have to decide you want a better relationship, a better marriage, or the professional career of your dreams. These things are attainable, but you must first make the decision. Whether you realize it or not, you are making a decision to settle every day that you choose to not go after what it is in life that you truly want. I want to give you practical tools to help empower you by reversing the settling decisions you're making and replacing them with positive, courageous decisions that will help you attain the professional life of your dreams.

Whether you are just starting in your professional career, or if you are looking to start over but you feel it may be too late, I want to let you know it's never too early and it's never too late to go after the things you want in your career. As long as you have life you have an opportunity to make a change. Don't let procrastination trick you into thinking you have time and you can wait, and don't let fear tell you it's too late. Get started......today! Remember this: while you were waiting for it, somebody else was working for it. While you were thinking about it, somebody was trying it. While you were deciding, somebody had already made a decision. You're behind because you won't make a decision. STOP SETTLING FOR LESS AND MAKE A DECISION TO GO GET MORE!!!

2
Entrepreneurship Versus a Career As An Employee

"It is not usual to speak of an employee as a partner, and yet what else is he?" – Henry Ford

Would you rather be an entrepreneur or work as an employee in a structured work environment? I've asked quite a few individuals to give me their answer to this question. Even though everyone has the choice, most of the people that I talk to are in a structured work environment. Many people's answer to my question is that they would rather be an entrepreneur... which then prompts me to ask them what product do they want to sell or what service can they provide. Most often the response is something they've seen someone else sell successfully or something they think they would be good at and enjoy.

After the initial question, I then proceed to ask why they want to be an entrepreneur. The first response I normally hear is they want to be able to make as much money as they want. I then ask, "How much money do you want to make, and more importantly, what is the number you need to be able to live comfortably and do all the things you want to do financially for yourself, your family, and to be able to give to any cause you feel strongly about?" Most don't have the answer to that question.

Many people say they want more money, but I think it is important to know how much you need to live the life you want to live. It's all a part of having a target to aim for and something to work towards.

When a person tells me they want to make six figures, I respond, "Six figures is a wide range, so you need to be more specific." That usually gets people thinking.

I also ask if the number can be accomplished as an employee. Some say "yes," but they normally follow their response up with reasons why they wouldn't be able to reach that level. Others say "no" without giving it much thought.

For those that say they can't reach that level, I like to have a conversation as to the reasons why they feel that way. The most common answer I receive is, "Those levels are only reserved for a select few." Well, the same can be said about those that are making an extreme amount of money in the entrepreneurial world, but that doesn't stop people from having a dream and even pursuing entrepreneurship. So why should that stop you from pursuing those levels as an employee? The answer is, most people aren't willing to put in the work to achieve that level of success. That is the same reason why many don't achieve the massive amount of success in the entrepreneurial world.

The second response I receive about wanting to be an entrepreneur is being able to take off whenever they want and not have to ask anyone for permission. Well, as an entrepreneur you still have a responsibility to your customers, and starting out, even years after starting, you still may not be able to take off when you want to if your business is not at a point where you can afford to have the doors closed or a staff that is able to run the business while you are gone.

Most people I have this conversation with are looking at the people at the top of a particular field of entrepreneurship. They want the success they see, but not the struggle that most had to go through to get there. There are great stories for those that have great success as entrepreneurs. Along with those great stories there are also stories of struggle and sacrifice for years before they reached the level of success that everyone sees and many are attracted to.

After going through all of that, I leave them with this: "To achieve a high level of success, you are going to have to go through some sacrifice." It doesn't matter which side you are doing it on, entrepreneur or employee, the question is always *Are you willing to go through what it takes to get there?*

There are many people who think being an entrepreneur is the only way to have career and financial success, and to enjoy what they do for a living. I know individuals who have built successful careers, who love what they do, and who have also become millionaires, all while working in a structured work environment as an employee.

I also like to tell the story of a person I knew and was able to help become an entrepreneur as an owner operator truck driver. He left his job as an employee truck driver and wanted to own his own truck and be his own boss. He lasted about three months. He was a great truck driver, but he was unsuccessful when it came to being the boss. I even paired him with a friend who did the same thing, but he was still unsuccessful. He just couldn't grasp the concept of knowing what he should or should not do, what loads he should or should not take, and what he needed to do in order to make money.

After about three months, he returned the truck and said he was going back to the company he left as an employee truck driver. He needed to be in a structured work environment. His reason for wanting to be his own boss was because his friend, who we had also helped become an owner operator truck driver, had left the company and was doing well being his own boss. Because he saw his friend do it, he automatically thought he could do the same thing, and that being his own boss was the thing to do in order to achieve success. He quickly found out it wasn't as easy as he thought, and he went back to the structured environment he was comfortable with and successful.

I'm definitely not against entrepreneurship, and have started multiple businesses myself. Some have done well and some not so well. I will say that I don't think everyone is purposed to be an entrepreneur. If everyone is purposed to be an entrepreneur, then who would be left to actually do the work as an employee?

I do believe everyone has the potential to be great at something, and for quite a few people, that something is being a great employee. There is nothing wrong with that. In fact, if that is what they are purposed to do they are exactly where they should be for their career success.

3
CAREER SUCCESS

"Finding a ladder (steps) to success is the easy part. It's the climbing (work) that stops most people from getting there!" – *Edgar Butler, Jr.*

1. Describe your idea of career success?

One definition of success is: *The accomplishment of an aim or purpose.* Career success will not look the same for everyone. For some, it could be based on how much money they make, or their professional title. For some, it could be how they are able to use their talents and skills each day to add value. You have to know what success looks like for you to know what you are working for and how you plan to go about attaining it.

For me, career success means being able to utilize the leadership abilities I have to positively impact the lives of others each day, and to also be able to use the gift I've been given to motivate, inspire, and empower people to pursue their best personal and professional life.

I challenge you to align your career success with the talent and skills you possess. It will not only give you the satisfaction of accomplishing goals, but more importantly, it gives you a sense of fulfillment each day as you are able to use the gifts and talents you have been given.

1. **What does career success look like for you?**

___

As you look to attain career success, you have to self assess where you currently are. Many people lack the ability to self assess. They do not want to have a real moment with themselves to say where they truly are in their professional life. For the most part, many are not meeting the standard they either have set or the standard they want to achieve.

1. **On a scale of 1 – 10, (1 being the closest and 10 being the farthest) how close or how far are you from achieving career success?**

___

2. **What steps can you take today to start closing the gap?**

___

After self-assessing, the next step is to put a plan in place that will be your guide for closing the gap in your pursuit of career success. An Individual Development Plan is something I highly recommend. This will be your road map for how you plan to pursue your career success and achieve your career goals. I suggest meeting with your career mentor and having them to assist you. They will probably be able to pull some things out of you by asking you some tough questions which will help you put a solid plan in place from the start. You may have to make some adjustments along the way, which is perfectly fine, but you now have a visual that will help you focus on what needs to be done to reach your career goals.

In my career, I put together Individual Development Plans to help keep me on track with pursuing my career goals. I would revisit my plan and check off benchmarks along the way. It helped me to remain focused on my goals, and also gave me milestones that helped give me a sense of accomplishment as I moved towards the larger goals.

Use the templates on the following pages to help you create an Individual Development Plan.

Separate the goals by month and list them as the three most important things (MIT) you want to accomplish in each quarter. Since there are three months in each quarter, list one goal/MIT per month of each quarter. It is important to put a date on each goal/MIT to establish when it should be completed. Use the SMART (Specific, Measurable, Attainable, Relevant, Time-based) format when determining your goals/MITs. Share your plan with your career mentor or someone that will hold you accountable.

1st quarter

January goal/MIT:

What are four weekly activities/tasks that will put you in position to accomplish this?

1.

_____

2.

_____

3.

_____

4.

_____

February goal/MIT:

What are four weekly activities/tasks that will put you in position to accomplish this?

1.

_____

2.

_____

3.

_____

4.

_____

March goal/MIT:

What are four weekly activities/tasks that will put you in position to accomplish this?

1.

_____

2.

_____

3.

_____

4.

_____

2nd quarter

April goal/MIT:

What are four weekly activities/tasks that will put you in position to accomplish this?

1.

_____

2.

_____

3.

_____

4.

_____

May goal/MIT:

What are four weekly activities/tasks that will put you in position to accomplish this?

1.

2.

3.

4.

June goal/MIT:

What are four weekly activities/tasks that will put you in position to accomplish this?

1.

2.

3.

4.

3rd quarter

July goal/MIT:

What are four weekly activities/tasks that will put you in position to accomplish this?

1.

2.

3.

4.

August goal/MIT:

What are four weekly activities/tasks that will put you in position to accomplish this?

1.

2.

3.

4.

September goal/MIT:

What are four weekly activities/tasks that will put you in position to accomplish this?
1.

_____

2.

_____

3.

_____

4.

_____

4th quarter

October goal/MIT:

What are four weekly activities/tasks that will put you in position to accomplish this?
1.

_____

2.

_____

3.

_____

4.

_____

November goal/MIT:

What are four weekly activities/tasks that will put you in position to accomplish this?

1.

2.

3.

4.

December goal/MIT:

What are four weekly activities/tasks that will put you in position to accomplish this?

1.

2.

3.

4.

4
THE TWO "WHYS"

"When you feel like quitting think about why you started" -
Anonymous

You should have two "Whys" as it relates to your work: The "Why" you started working for the company, took the job, or started working in your profession, and the "Why" that keeps you going on the days you feel like quitting. The "Why" you got started will vary. You may have taken the job for financial reasons or for more opportunity. Maybe you have been out of the working environment for a while, and this was an opportunity to get back in. Whatever your reasons for starting, you constantly need to revisit that place to make sure your "Why" is still the same.

I remember when I took a four dollar pay cut to join State Farm. I didn't take the job because of the money. I took the job for opportunity. I was brought in at the entry level of entry levels! You may be asking yourself *what is entry level of entry levels*? I was told by the Human Resource Representative they wanted to bring me in at one entry level position, but because my typing words per minute didn't meet the minimum target, I didn't qualify for that position. The representative still wanted to bring me in, so they offered me another entry level position that didn't require much typing. Since I didn't qualify for initial entry level, the position I was offered had to be the entry level of entry levels! That never fazed me. As I mentioned earlier, my "Why" for joining State Farm was for opportunity.

Because I understood my reason for joining State Farm, I always kept that on the forefront of my mind, and it became one of my goals for going to work each day. I wasn't looking for instant success. I wanted the opportunity to show my skills and to apply my work ethic to get me to the position I wanted. Each day, I understood I was working towards my goal, so I took each day and made the most of it.

I have worked for State Farm for nine years and in those nine years, I have been in eight different positions. Overall, I have been offered ten different positions within the company. I turned down two positions because I was accepting another position at the same time. Again, I understood my "Why" for taking the position with the company and I took full advantage of the opportunities.

1. **When was the last time you revisited "Why" you took your current job?**

2. **Has your "Why" changed?**

3. **Does your "Why" still align with what is being offered in the organization?**

4. **If your "Why" has changed and no longer aligns with what is being offered in the organization, are you prepared to move?**

Whatever your "Why" is, you have to make sure the opportunity for you to accomplish the goal is still available where you are. If not, you have to prepare to move. The longer you stay, the further you fall away from accomplishing your goals.

Searching for a new career opportunity can be uncomfortable, especially if you've been with an organization for some years. You must realize your career growth and enjoyment will only be accomplished when you put yourself in proper position. To fulfill your career aspirations, you must place yourself within an environment that has opportunities that align with your "Why".

1. **List some benefits of working within your current organization.**

_____

_____

_____

_____

2. **List some things missing within your current organization that you need.**

_____

_____

_____

_____

Your second "Why" is what keeps you going on the days you feel like giving up. Everything won't go right every day. There are going to be tough days. It is on those days you need to remember the "Why" you do what you do in order for you to keep going. My family is my "Why" I do what I do. They depend on me to go out each day and put forth my best effort. I cannot expect to provide a certain quality of lifestyle if I do not give my best on a daily basis. I cannot be ok with telling my family there are certain things we can't do and know that I did not give my best to put us in the best financial situation. So, each day I give my all to make sure I never have to have that type of conversation. I expect for my kids and my wife to give their best, and I don't expect any less from myself. In fact, I expect more from myself.

My youngest daughter was born with a cyst on her brain. We were told she would have mental and physical limitations. After multiple surgeries on her head before her first birthday, she has defied all the negative reports given by the doctors. She is an A/B student and has played multiple sports. She is our miracle from God! She gives her all in everything she does to prove the doctors wrong. When I see how hard she tries, it gives me fuel to keep pushing, no matter how tough things get. The "Why" you do what you do will get you through the tough days and into better days. If you keep hanging on to better days, those better days will eventually turn into your best days.

1. **What or who is your "Why" you do what you do?**

2. Why is this your "Why"?

_____

_____

_____

_____

_____

_____

_____

_____

_____

3. Describe times you can think of when you kept going because of your "Why"?

_____

_____

_____

_____

_____

_____

_____

_____

_____

THE 3 C'S IN LIFE: CHOICE, CHANCE, CHANGE.
YOU MUST MAKE A CHOICE, TO TAKE A CHANCE, OR YOUR LIFE WILL NEVER CHANGE. - ANONYMOUS

List some areas in your career that you have been on the fence about or have not been pursuing with your all. Then, state how you are going to make a decision to go after what you truly want:

1.

2.

3.

1.

2.

3.

5
JOB VERSUS CAREER

"A job is something you get; a career is something you build!" – Edgar Butler, Jr.

A job is something you get; a career is something you build! When you view what you do as a job, in your mind you're thinking, "I can easily get another one of these," and you take it for granted. A job is something that is viewed as a temporary place of employment until you can find something better. A career is something you build over time with the intentions of it being long-term.

In your current position, did you go in thinking of it as a career or a job? This definitely has an impact on how you go about your work on a daily basis. If you view where you're at as just a job, you are not giving your maximum effort because you don't value what you do.

When you view your work as a career, you mentally invest yourself into what you are doing, and you feel your work means something. You value what you do. When you value what you do, you take pride in your work and you give your best on a daily basis. You view your work as having meaning, and you look at it as being impactful to the purpose you serve. The longer you are in a job instead of a career, the longer you delay reaching your professional goals.

When you are in a job, you don't look for opportunities where you are. You think your time there is limited and you are only there to pass the time. But, without a plan to move to a career, what you currently view as a job, over time, actually becomes your career. This is definitely a problem because you will not look for opportunities to increase your salary or for promotions that could get you to a place to utilize your skills and which will allow you to operate in your gifts and talents. This also delays you from getting to the place you need to be to benefit those you are doing it for. Remember your "Whys"! Your "Whys" need you to get to your goal because they will benefit. Can you honestly say you would be ok with letting them down?

1. **Are you currently in a job or your career?**

_____

2. **If you are currently in a job are you ready to seek and find your career?**

_____

3. **What do you want to pursue as a career?**

_____

_____

_____

_____

4. What is stopping you from pursuing your career?

5. In your current work environment, is there an opportunity for you to turn your job into a career?

6. What action can you take today to move you closer to your career?

When I joined State Farm, I knew from the first day I was starting my career. Everything up to that point was only a job. I was now going to a place where I could utilize my skills, increase my salary, and take advantage of many professional opportunities. Although I didn't have any insurance experience, I knew my work ethic would take me places experience alone could not. Prior to my first day on the job, I promised myself that I would give my all each day to put myself in a position to advance and be successful. I didn't take a work day off for the first six months. Remember, I was used to working five and six days a week, for 10 and 12 hour days, starting at four and five o'clock in the morning, and all physical labor. My schedule with State Farm was Monday through Friday, 8:00am to 4:30pm, and sitting at a desk all day. I had the weekends off, and my work ethic was so strong I didn't feel a need to take any additional days off. Everyone's situation is different, so I'm not saying everyone should do that, but it was something I was able to do, and it was a part of my plan to reach my goals.

Attack the day; don't let the day attack you!

Each day you should be creating small wins. The small wins help you build momentum that lead to larger wins. Many people often think that when one thing happens during their day that doesn't go as planned, their entire day is ruined. That's because many people don't set daily goals to accomplish.

My coach uses the term small wins to describe accomplishing daily goals. When you look to accomplish small wins, even when things come along and disrupt your day, you can still end the day feeling like you've won because you've accomplished the things you set out to accomplish that day.

I've seen it many times: a person has a flat tire on their way to work and when that happens, they have mentally lost the day because they didn't set a goal to accomplish. If a goal is set and you accomplish the goal, dealing with the flat tire just becomes a hurdle that you cleared on your way to the goal.

Daily goals (Small wins!) Start listing daily goals you want to accomplish each workday that will become your small wins.

Monday:

Tuesday:

Wednesday:

Thursday:

Friday:

Saturday:

Sunday:

Don't stop dreaming!

So many employees that I talk to have lost their desire to dream. You should never lose your desire to dream! Even in a structured work environment, your ideas are still needed. The company needs your ideas to help them move the company forward. Every successful company attained and maintained their success because of the ideas and the work of the team members in the company. I have found that many team members box themselves in to the description of the position they hold, and they do not think outside of that box. If their job is to build widgets, that is what they do with no deviation. If they are packaging or showing merchandise, that is what they do with no deviation. Even some people in leadership only think about managing what's in front of them and they never really focus on leading. Think beyond your title. Your title is the description of what you do. Allow your skill-set to become what you do. I truly want you to think about the term "think outside the box", and then I want you to start applying it!

6

THE POWER
WITHIN!

"Don't let the fear of competition stop you. Get in the game and make the competition fear you!" – Edgar Butler, Jr.

You have POWER, but have you activated it? Everyone has power, but some have not activated their power to help get them to the level they would like to be at for their career. Let's break down POWER and what you need to do to activate it.

P - Prioritize
O – Opportunities
W – Work while you wait
E – Effort
R – Remember who and what you are doing it for!

Prioritize

The first thing you need to do is to Prioritize. You need to prioritize what matters in your career. This goes back to Chapter 4 when we discussed the two "Whys". There are things in our life that matter more than others. There should also be things in our career that matter more than others. This will be different for many people. For some, it may be extrinsic. For others, it may be more intrinsic. It could be more money, a higher title, or increased opportunities. It could be the satisfaction of completing projects, the impact your work has in the community, or the lives of people you help. Whatever it is, you need to identify it as a priority. Know what is important to you in the work you do each day. When you prioritize what's important in your career, you can provide greater attention to detail for meeting your career goals.

Make a Priority list from 1 – 3 of things that are important for you to achieve in your career, with 1 being the most important and 3 being the least important.

1.

_____

2.

_____

3.

_____

The next component of Prioritizing requires you to prioritize your day. Many people that I have led and coached have no structure to their day. To become the most efficient and effective at what you do, you need to create a system that allows you to operate at your maximum potential each day.

I was listening to CJ Quinney (from Eric Thomas & Associates) at a workshop, and he talked about the power of having home field advantage. He mentioned he did some research and saw that 22 out of the 32 teams in the NFL in the 2016 season had a better home record than they did away. He said he reached out to an NFL friend and tried to get some answers as to why this was. His friend told him when they are away they have so many distractions that they can't totally focus on the game. He said they spend hours on the field changing cleats to make sure they have the best ones. They are sleeping in a hotel and the bed may not be to their comfort level. He said their routine for the time they get home and get to bed could be totally thrown off because they are out of town. The player said when they are home all of those things are not distractions and they can focus solely on playing the game. Then, CJ said he took that and said he needed to create home field advantage in his business, so he started working from home because he knew that is where he could minimize the distractions and operate at his highest level. I also took that same concept and applied it to my business by creating home field advantage in our careers each day.

If you prioritize your workday, you should be be able to create a routine for how you spend your time. From the time you wake up until the time you go to sleep, you should know exactly what you are supposed to be doing. You may have to make adjustments along the way, but this will give you some structure to help keep you on task and also allow you to maximize your time each day. Start out by tracking what you do throughout your workday, each day, for five consecutive days. Use 30 minute intervals to help you laser your focus and not create too many gaps in time.

Use the template on the upcoming pages to help you track your day for five consecutive days. You may need to alter the times depending on your work schedule.

Day 1

TIME	ACTIVITY
7:00 A.M.	
7:30 A.M.	
8:00 A.M.	
8:30 A.M.	
9:00 A.M.	
9:30 A.M.	
10:00 A.M.	
10:30 A.M.	
11:00 A.M.	
11:30 A.M.	
12:00 P.M.	

TIME	ACTIVITY
12:30 P.M.	
1:00 P.M.	
1:30 P.M.	
2:00 P.M.	
2:30 P.M.	
3:00 P.M.	
3:30 P.M.	
4:00 P.M.	
4:30 P.M.	
5:00 P.M.	
5:30 P.M.	

Day 2

TIME	ACTIVITY
7:00 A.M.	
7:30 A.M.	
8:00 A.M.	
8:30 A.M.	
9:00 A.M.	
9:30 A.M.	
10:00 A.M.	
10:30 A.M.	
11:00 A.M.	
11:30 A.M.	
12:00 P.M.	

TIME	ACTIVITY
12:30 P.M.	
1:00 P.M.	
1:30 P.M.	
2:00 P.M.	
2:30 P.M.	
3:00 P.M.	
3:30 P.M.	
4:00 P.M.	
4:30 P.M.	
5:00 P.M.	
5:30 P.M.	

Day 3

TIME	ACTIVITY
7:00 A.M.	
7:30 A.M.	
8:00 A.M.	
8:30 A.M.	
9:00 A.M.	
9:30 A.M.	
10:00 A.M.	
10:30 A.M.	
11:00 A.M.	
11:30 A.M.	
12:00 P.M.	

TIME	ACTIVITY
12:30 P.M.	
1:00 P.M.	
1:30 P.M.	
2:00 P.M.	
2:30 P.M.	
3:00 P.M.	
3:30 P.M.	
4:00 P.M.	
4:30 P.M.	
5:00 P.M.	
5:30 P.M.	

Day 4

TIME	ACTIVITY
7:00 A.M.	
7:30 A.M.	
8:00 A.M.	
8:30 A.M.	
9:00 A.M.	
9:30 A.M.	
10:00 A.M.	
10:30 A.M.	
11:00 A.M.	
11:30 A.M.	
12:00 P.M.	

TIME	ACTIVITY
12:30 P.M.	
1:00 P.M.	
1:30 P.M.	
2:00 P.M.	
2:30 P.M.	
3:00 P.M.	
3:30 P.M.	
4:00 P.M.	
4:30 P.M.	
5:00 P.M.	
5:30 P.M.	

Day 5

TIME	ACTIVITY
7:00 A.M.	
7:30 A.M.	
8:00 A.M.	
8:30 A.M.	
9:00 A.M.	
9:30 A.M.	
10:00 A.M.	
10:30 A.M.	
11:00 A.M.	
11:30 A.M.	
12:00 P.M.	

TIME	ACTIVITY
12:30 P.M.	
1:00 P.M.	
1:30 P.M.	
2:00 P.M.	
2:30 P.M.	
3:00 P.M.	
3:30 P.M.	
4:00 P.M.	
4:30 P.M.	
5:00 P.M.	
5:30 P.M.	

After you track your day for five consecutive days, create a system, schedule, or routine that will allow you to reduce wasted time and maximize the time you have each workday. You can use the template on pages 67 and 68 to capture what you should be doing throughout each work day and push yourself to follow the system you create. Assess your system and make adjustments until you have a system in place that keeps you on task for maximum performance.

To help you get started, here are some things to think about. If you work at a desk, make sure you have your desk set up and ready to go by a certain time each day. Put your chair in the right place, adjust your desk height if that is an option, have your computer screens at the right angle, put your phone in the place you need to allow the best accessibility and comfort, have all your items such as pencils, pens, stationery, paper clips, stapler, etc. all stocked and ready to go! If you need beverages and/or snacks, make sure you have them also stocked and ready to go! These things seem small, but anything that can help you become more efficient is what we want to accomplish.

If your place of employment is not an office, you still need to create a routine, schedule, or strategy for maximizing your day. Look for the inefficiencies in your workday and then look for opportunities to become more efficient. Have all of your necessities in order and make sure they are set in proper place. This will help reduce your transition time, which will transfer into greater efficiency.

My System (Daily Routine)

TIME	ACTIVITY
7:00 A.M.	
7:30 A.M.	
8:00 A.M.	
8:30 A.M.	
9:00 A.M.	
9:30 A.M.	
10:00 A.M.	
10:30 A.M.	
11:00 A.M.	
11:30 A.M.	
12:00 P.M.	

TIME	ACTIVITY
12:30 P.M.	
1:00 P.M.	
1:30 P.M.	
2:00 P.M.	
2:30 P.M.	
3:00 P.M.	
3:30 P.M.	
4:00 P.M.	
4:30 P.M.	
5:00 P.M.	
5:30 P.M.	

<u>Opportunities –Find the gaps!</u>

In the company I work for, there isn't a job description or title for someone to go around and motivate and inspire team members throughout the organization. It was noted that morale was down in some areas of the company. I viewed that as my opportunity to utilize my talent and create value for the company by helping to increase the morale. Some people felt that was the responsibility of the leader over the team. I felt it was the responsibility of anyone who had that talent and ability. I was that person!

I began asking other leaders if I could come and share my career story and help motivate and inspire their team through workshops and empowerment sessions. My approach was not one of filling a void, but more so an addition to what the leader was already doing with their team. It wasn't received openly by everyone, but many leaders opened their doors and allowed me to come in. I presented at team meetings and even led workshops for my leadership peers and upper leadership. I did presentations in different departments as well as my own. The word began to spread, and I realized there was a need for the service I was providing.

I use my experience as an example when talking to individuals, teams, and other organizations. I created a lane for myself within a structured environment!

Opportunities – If it's not there, create it!

Sometimes opportunities may not be readily available within your current work environment. That doesn't mean there aren't opportunities for you to create opportunities. Take your skills and put them to use! Use your skills to create the career you want. In order for this to work, you must show how the position or project will benefit the team, department, and/or organization. Look for gaps and find ways to use your skills to fill those gaps.

For example, if information needs to be shared on each team, but currently each team has to collect the information and then someone on each team has to draft an email or letter to send to the team, if you have writing skills you could propose collecting the information, formatting a newsletter and submitting the information out to each team on a routine basis. This gives you the opportunity to showcase your writing skills to multiple people within the department. You would then utilize that opportunity to springboard you to other opportunities within the organization. Think of every opportunity as an opportunity for the next opportunity. This will keep you creating opportunities and looking for opportunities.

Understand the talent you have and how you can leverage your talent to create opportunities within the organization. Remember, if the lane is not there, create it!

I had a team member that I was leading and I mentioned that I wanted them to utilize their talent more. They told me it was easier for them to do when there were certain programs and systems in place that would allow them to gather data. I asked, "If it's not there, what's stopping you from creating a system or program?" I was letting them know they had the skill-set to create a program, so stop waiting for the opportunity to be given to them and go out and create the opportunity. They listened, put together a presentation, and was able to present it to upper leadership, which created additional exposure for them and led to other opportunities. I will say it again, if the lane is not there, create it!

1. **List a skill-set or talent you have that is not being utilized in your day to day work.**

2. List areas (gaps) within the company that you can fill by utilizing your talent. For example, if you are a writer, can you begin to gather valuable information that can be shared with other team members in the organization through some form of written communication?

3. How can you use your talent to add value to the company in a way not currently being recognized?

4. In what way would you like to use your talent/skills?

5. What is stopping you?

_____

_____

_____

_____

6. What steps can you take immediately to start utilizing your talent/skills?

_____

_____

_____

_____

Work while you wait!

Ok, so the major promotion is not there yet or the big project is not there yet… so what do you do? You work while you wait. You can't wait until you see the opportunity to start working for it; you have to start working now and continue working each day. As you continue to work each day, you fully prepare yourself for the opportunity before it opens up.

You can outwork your competition by continuously working. I've seen many people miss out on opportunities because they were not prepared. They waited until the promotion was posted and then started trying to put things together to help them prepare for the interview or project. If you focus on the work, you don't worry about the wait.

When I decided to make my work the priority, I didn't get discouraged during the wait. I knew I was building my portfolio and giving myself an advantage while others were only waiting. I would hear team members say, "I'm waiting for them to post........." I would say to myself, "Great!" because I knew while they were waiting, I would be working, and my work would provide me with the necessary answers I needed during interview time. My work would provide me with business results that I could speak to during evaluations, and it would give me consistent visibility before choices were being made for projects. You can either separate yourself from the competition or stay with the crowd. It depends on whether you are willing to work or just wait.

Effort!

Usually when we start a new career at a new place of employment, we go in with a lot of excitement and energy. We have plans to be the best at what we do and plans to rise to the top. We start out of the gate fast and strong! After we've settled, and things become familiar, the excitement and energy fades, and so does our effort.

1.   **On a scale from 1 – 10 (1 being the lowest and 10 being the highest) how would you honestly rate your level of effort today?**

If you didn't answer 10 that's ok; it just says you have work to do. This is a part of self-assessing.

To achieve those big goals and big dreams, we not only have to maintain our excitement and energy, but our effort has to increase. There are different levels that must be achieved before we reach the top. As we continue to ascend to each different level, our effort has to match and then exceed for us to go higher.

When I started with State Farm as an Imaging Processor, I never let my position control my level of effort. I understood that if I was going to make it to a Leadership position my effort needed to match where I was going and not where I was at the time. The key players in the organization need to be able to see you in the role you are trying to get before they give it to you. Remember, it's never about the title, but always about the way you carry yourself each day.

1. **If you were doing the hiring, would you give you a raise or promotion based on the effort you see from you each day?**

Your effort should be fueled by your desire to get to where you want to be in your career. This is where you will also have to be able to block out the noise of those that are giving minimum effort. They will try to detract you from giving your best.

First they will ask you why you are doing it.....but later they will ask you how you did it! – Unknown

How do you increase your level of effort? You focus on increasing and doing a little more each day. My coach likes to say, "Give 1% more each day." I like to say, be consistently better each day than you were the day before.

Earlier in the book, I talked about self-assessing. In order for you to be better than you were the day before, you have to know where you were the day before. That comes from self-assessing. Look back at your day and identify the things you did great and the areas you can improve. Now, look to see how you increase your effort in the areas to improve without diminishing in the things you did that were great.

If you truly want to be at your best and operate at your highest level, you have to be willing to identify your areas of weakness and strengthen them.

To give yourself a mental boost, I tell people to give your best effort each day as if your employment tomorrow depended on what you do today. We tend to take our employment for granted and assume it is a given that we will be allowed to come back tomorrow. This is when those that have a desire to be an entrepreneur usually tell me this is one of the reasons why they would rather be an entrepreneur. Just because you are an entrepreneur doesn't mean you will always have customers buying your products. Times change, and as a business owner, if you don't change with the times you could find yourself out of business.

As an entrepreneur you have to give your customers what they want, and as an employee you have to give the company what they want. In both situations you should pride yourself on the work that you do, and you should be giving your best in both circumstances.

If you want to receive maximum reward, give maximum effort and do great work. On the flip side, if you are giving minimum effort and not so great work, you shouldn't look to receive maximum reward.

Remember who and what you are doing it for!

This goes back to your "Whys". When you are doing it for someone or something other than yourself you tend to push farther, endure longer, fight harder and give more.

The Six P Principles!

Potential will get you in the door, but it is your Performance, being able to Prove your performance, and you remaining Positive that will get you to Pay and Promotion.

If you are being looked at for a CEO or high ranking Executive position most likely, there will need to be some prior evidence of you being able to fill that position successfully, and there will be a higher level of expectation. If you are being considered for any position lower than that you are mainly being hired based on the potential you have to fill the role successfully. At some point, you will be expected to fulfill the potential the company saw in you. If you are unable to meet their standards and expectations, don't expect to receive additional pay, bonuses, or promotions. You have to be able to live up to the potential.

Living up to the potential means performing at the level the company expected when they hired you.

That means you have to perform, and also be able to show proof of your performance. Quotas and metrics have to be met, and if you want to receive higher bonuses and compensation, they have to be exceeded. You can't just say you've been doing a great job; it must be measured and shown to provide proof. When it's evidenced, you have something to stand on when presenting your case for why you should receive additional pay or a promotion.

You also have to remain positive! Getting the extra pay or promotion may not happen right away. You can't allow that to take away from the positive things you've done by having a negative attitude. Now, that doesn't mean you have to put up with it forever, but it may take some time to manifest. Raises and promotions may only happen during specific times of the year. Make sure you understand the process, and if you don't you should ask. Whatever you do, don't allow your frustration to cause you to erase all of your hard work by becoming negative. I don't know of many, if any, problems that get solved by being negative.

After you're hired, don't continue to look for grace based on your potential. Start performing and making sure you can prove your performance. Always maintain a positive attitude. Then you will start to build a bridge to get you to increased pay and promotion.

7

DEDICATE
YOURSELF

"Dedication and commitment are what transfer dreams into realities." – Unknown

In order for you to reach success in your career, you must dedicate yourself to your decisions. Without dedication, you will likely quit when things are not going the way you planned. When times get hard, you will likely walk away from your decision or settle for less. It's not to say that some decisions are not the right decision, and you may need to change course, but if you have thought the decision through and have decided to make a move, you have to give your decision a fighting chance. Your decision won't stand a chance if you are not dedicated to it.

1. **Again, write out what you want to pursue as your career.**

_____

_____

_____

2. **On a scale from 1 – 10 (1 being the least and 10 being the most) how dedicated are you to pursuing your career?**

_____

As I mentioned in chapter one, when I joined State Farm, I literally started at one of the most entry level positions in the company. This also meant that my pay was a lot lower than what I was previously making. Four dollars an hour lower to be exact. My yearly salary was $20,600. Even though we had a house payment, two children, and the other entire household bills and expenses, I dedicated myself to the decision I made. I looked at the opportunities for success within the company, I made a decision to join, and I dedicated myself to the decision. There were definitely tough financial times that required our family to shuffle around bills, make some payments late, skip some payments, and asking for forgiveness of some debts. I still did not let that stop me from sticking with the decision I had made.

As I'm writing this book and thinking back on those times, I can honestly say it was all worth it! Making a decision to become successful is the start, but that's not where things end. You truly have to be dedicated to your decision. There are going to be times when people will call you crazy for sticking with the decision, but your belief in the decision will help fuel your dedication.

I believed in my decision to move past the entry level position I was in when I started with the company and I dedicated myself to the pursuit of formal Leadership. Were there tough days? Yes. Did everything go the way I planned from day one? No, but regardless of how things looked from one day to the next, I never lost my dedication. In your career, you have to be dedicated and willing to hang in there through some of the ups and downs. Your dedication is also an indication of how much you want to see career success. Some days you may barely be staying afloat. Even then, you have to be dedicated to your decision if your decision is one that involves you reaching success.

Frank Lloyd Wright once said, "I know the price of success: Dedication, hard work and an unremitting devotion to the things you want to see happen." This is so very true! Without dedication, you will not last through the tests and trials that are sure to come. Along with your decision, prepare your mind for dedication through the highs and lows, the yes and no's, the sure and the unsure. Embrace the process and not the results. As you embrace the process, you become more dedicated to the decision.

List some potential roadblocks that you can anticipate. Then, list how you can potentially remove or overcome those roadblocks. Being proactive will help you prepare for what you may face and will help your dedication if you anticipate what's to come.

1.

2.

3.

1.

2.

3.

8
DISCIPLINE

"Discipline is doing what needs to be done, even if you don't want to do it." – Unknown

There are going to be things in your career that are going to happen that can deter you from your goals and dreams. This is where your discipline has to kick in. People may come and go. Business deals may fall apart. Your friends may want to hang out and party when you have work to do. People will try to promote negativity to get you to look at things in a negative way. "They are always making changes at the job." "They don't pay us enough, so why should I care." You have to be disciplined enough to block out the noise and negativity and stay focused.

Know that you are a part of influencing the environment. You are either positively or negatively contributing to the environment. You create what you want to see and the environment you want to be in each day.

Don't allow pursuit of the goals you have for yourself to be thrown off course because you are around others that don't have those same goals and desires. Many people will say they want to achieve certain things, but when it comes time to put in the work, they settle for average. Separate yourself from those that don't have your same desire for career advancement and growth. If you don't, you could hurt yourself just by association, or by mentally changing your focus because you start to conform to the average behavior of those you are around.

Build relationships of value and on purpose. Ones that add value to you and ones you can add value to. The second one you may have to approach with caution so you don't end up trying to pour into someone who is not willing to receive and they end up tarnishing your brand in the process.

In my pursuit of leadership, I knew there were things I needed to do to make sure I met the expectations set by the company. Beyond that, I had expectations for myself. Some of the company's expectations were arriving on time, leaving on time, coming back from break and lunch on time, being at the desk working, continuously getting better at my job and completing my work, being at work when scheduled, acting professional, dressing professional, and being a team player.

My expectations for myself included arriving early, staying late, coming back from break and lunch early, always at the desk working, always at work when scheduled, becoming the best version of myself and being the best on the team, not only acting and dressing as a professional, but acting and dressing as a professional leader even though I hadn't made it to leadership yet. No excuses. I didn't want anything to be held against me. I said to myself, *if I can meet all the expectations of the company, then there would never be a reason for my leaders to tell me no when I wanted to pursue a different position or pursue a promotion.* My discipline kept me out of trouble and in the spotlight as a role model. I didn't just want to meet the standard; I wanted to be the standard!

1. **List some things you can start doing to set yourself a part from everyone else.**

_____

_____

_____

_____

_____

_____

When it's easy to slack off, your discipline will keep you doing the things that are necessary for you to get ahead. Everyone puts on their best show during the interview and makes promises that many do not keep. One definition of integrity is: *The quality of being honest and having strong moral principles; moral uprightness.* Your discipline will help you maintain your integrity by keeping your word for all the great things you said you would do during the interview.

Exhibit integrity in your work and in your relationships every day.

List some things you said you would do in your career that you have yet to do or have stopped doing that you need to continue? Then, write how you will go about accomplishing those things or getting back on track.

1.

2.

3.

1.

2.

3.

9
DETERMINATION

"Greatness doesn't give out invitations...you have to want it bad enough to crash the party!!!" - *Edgar Butler, Jr.*

You have made a decision to pursue your goals and dreams. You are dedicated to your decision. You are disciplined. Now, things start to get tough in the process. The days are long, the money is short, the bills are due, and the promotion hasn't come yet. They keep making changes on the job. What do you do? You keep showing up, you keep pushing, you keep grinding, and you keep working! You keep showing up on time. You continue to smile. You continue to communicate. You remain focused.

When I made my decision to pursue a corporate career, I said I was not going to let anything stop me from reaching my goal. I knew I would have to work harder than everyone else and I was ok with that. My typing wasn't great, and I knew I was going to have to take a typing test just to get in the door. So, every day leading up to the interview, I would go home and practice typing using free typing courses online. I barely passed the test. I told the HR rep if she just gave me a chance, my work ethic would take care of the rest. She said, "I see something in you, and I think that you would be a great fit for the company." I went through a second round of interviews and was hired.

I came in with people that had more talent. Some knew people in higher positions. Some had parents that knew people in higher positions. Some had college degrees from major universities. Here I was with a two year degree from a community college. I didn't know anyone in a high ranking position, and my mom didn't know anyone in a high ranking position. But, I had something they didn't. A will and a work ethic that was relentless! Where they relied on talent, I relied on drive and determination. Where they relied on who they knew, I was working hard to make sure as many people as possible knew me. Where they relied on their degree, I relied on my work ethic.

I did eventually get my Bachelor's degree.....18 years after I graduated from high school. It took me nine years after I graduated high school to complete my Associates degree and another nine years after that to complete my Bachelors. This is another example which shows it's never too late to go after what you want! I made sure I put myself in a position so when the door of opportunity was opened, I was the first face they saw. On my breaks, I would walk around in other departments of the company, eventually knowing I would find someone to have a conversation with and eventually create a networking opportunity. I went above and beyond the expectations to put myself in the best possible position.

I didn't always reach the goal on the first attempt, but I never gave up. I remember interviewing for a leadership promotion and I didn't get the position. I didn't get discouraged. I asked for feedback so I could understand the reasons why I wasn't chosen. They provided me with feedback and I thanked them. In my mind, they had just helped me prepare for the next opportunity. I took the feedback letter and pinned it on the wall in my cubicle. I said to myself *the next time these will no longer be reasons*. I was going to make sure I made the adjustments so they wouldn't be able to use those same reasons when I interviewed again. I interviewed for the same position about a year later and this time I got the offer! I was determined to not let anything stop me, and anytime I was rejected for a position I worked even harder to let everyone know I belonged there.

My dedication, discipline and determination continued to pay off! I went from just barely making it in, to being in a position that hired others. I don't say that to brag, but I say that to say my work ethic and determination have positioned me to take advantage of opportunities when they were presented.

You may have already experienced some rejection in your career. Don't allow that to deter you from the goal. Be willing to make the adjustments necessary to get to where you want to be. One thing I've discovered in talks with some people is it's easier for them to make an excuse than it is for them to make an adjustment. But I say, winners don't make excuses, we make adjustments, and then we make a way!

1. Write out again what you want to pursue as your career.

_____

2. On a scale of 1 – 10 (1 being the least and 10 being the most) how determined are you to accomplish your career goals?

_____

3. Have you positioned yourself to take advantage of the opportunity when it presents?

_____

4. If not, what steps can you take today to start positioning yourself?

_____

_____

_____

_____

_____

5. If your answer to question 3 is yes, what steps can you take to stay ready and continue to prepare yourself even more for the opportunity?

_____

_____

_____

_____

_____

_____

_____

_____

_____

_____

_____

On a scale of 1 – 10 (1 being the farthest and 10 being the closest) how close are you to being at your best in your career?

1   2   3   4   5   6   7   8   9   10

If you are not at 10, what steps can you implement today to start working your way towards 10?

1.

2.

3.

4.

5.

10
DOMINATE YOUR LANE!

"Be so good they can't ignore you." – Steve Martin

Dominating your lane comes when you focus on becoming the best version of you and then becoming the best at what you do! Dominating your lane is positioning yourself in a way that when the door of opportunity opens, your face is the first one seen. Dominating your lane means to position yourself in a way that others are thinking of ways to get you on their team, to a better place, or in a promoted position before anything is even available. Dominating your lane is giving more than what they asked for because you know eventually you will receive more in return. When you are looking to get ahead, get to the next level, or get to a better place, you have to be ready and willing to dominate your lane.

Don't look to meet the standard, be the standard! Go above the expectations and be the exception.

1. Are you currently dominating your lane?

2. If not, what steps can you take today to start working towards domination?

If you are in your career, dominating your lane means that if they post only one position for a promotion, the position has to be for you. You have to work each day as if they are only going to post one position for promotion. Others may hope that they post more than one position because they are thinking that will give them a better chance, but when you are dominating your lane you don't care if they only post one position because you know that position is for you! For this to be true, you have to give your all each day. Not giving your best each day cannot be an option. You have to understand that for you, every day is an interview, and you are building your resume' every day.

Many people go into an internal interview hoping the interviewers select them based on what they do in the 45 minutes to an hour they are in the interview. When you dominate your lane, you go into the interview knowing that you have worked for this opportunity every day, and you have been interviewing for them every day, so for you the interview is just an opportunity for you to gift wrap what they already know about you, and that is, you are the best person for the position.

Dominating your lane is all about outworking any and all competition. When I mentioned I've held eight different positions in the nine years I've been with the company and that I've been offered a total of ten different positions in nine years, people say "wow". I say "No, work". My mentality was that I was going to outwork any and all competition so when the opportunities became available, my name was the first one that came up in the conversation. Whenever I was asked to do something, I went above and beyond. I exceeded expectations. I networked on my breaks and lunch to build my relationships. I thought of ways to make my team and the department better. I made myself available and made sure I was accountable.

I worked hard to make sure I was the one they wanted, and if there was only one position available, I made sure I was at the top of their list. God told me to put in the work and He would open the doors. That's what I did. I didn't worry about what anyone else was doing, or what anyone else was saying. I did what I needed to do and I left the rest up to God.

You have what it takes to dominate your lane, but if you're not willing to compete you will not be able to move to the level of success available to you. To get to the top requires work. To become great requires work. To become the best, you have to outwork the best. Greatness is inside of each and every person, but it is those that are willing to work as hard as they can that find themselves achieving the level of greatness that seems unreachable to others. Greatness is inside of you, and it's waiting to be unleashed! You've held it in long enough. Let it go and begin to experience the career you've been dreaming about!

IT'S YOUR CAREER. TAKE CONTROL OF IT!!!

Notes

Notes

Notes

Notes

Notes

Notes

ABOUT THE AUTHOR

Edgar Butler, Jr. is a passionate speaker, mentor, and coach. He has worked in various areas of the business world including warehouses, fast food, entrepreneurship, and Corporate America. After working various jobs, and also being fired, he was given an opportunity to join the corporate world working for the #1 P&C Insurer in the United States. With a relentless work ethic and a desire to succeed, he quickly climbed the corporate ladder. In his first nine years, he held eight different positions starting from entry level and working his way up to Leadership. As a corporate leader, he's led teams responsible for managing multi-million dollar books of business.

Edgar's passion for helping others become their best has allowed him to impact lives in all walks of life through coaching, corporate training, professional development workshops, and student empowerment sessions. He serves as a leader in both his professional and personal life. He's a corporate leader, business owner, youth teacher, mentor and volunteer. To sum it up best, he's a servant leader.